Sometimes...

Letting Go Is the Beginning

Sometimes...Letting Go Is the Beginning

Printed in the United States of America
First Edition Printing

Front Cover Photos by Rob Dutton
Back Cover Photos by Anne L. Lanier

Design by
Arbor Services, Inc.
http://www.arborservices.co/

Sometimes...Letting Go Is the Beginning
Anne L. Lanier

ISBN: 979-8-234-08499-6

LCCN: 2026913675

1. Title 2. Author 3. Poetry

Sometimes…

Letting Go Is the Beginning

Anne L. Lanier

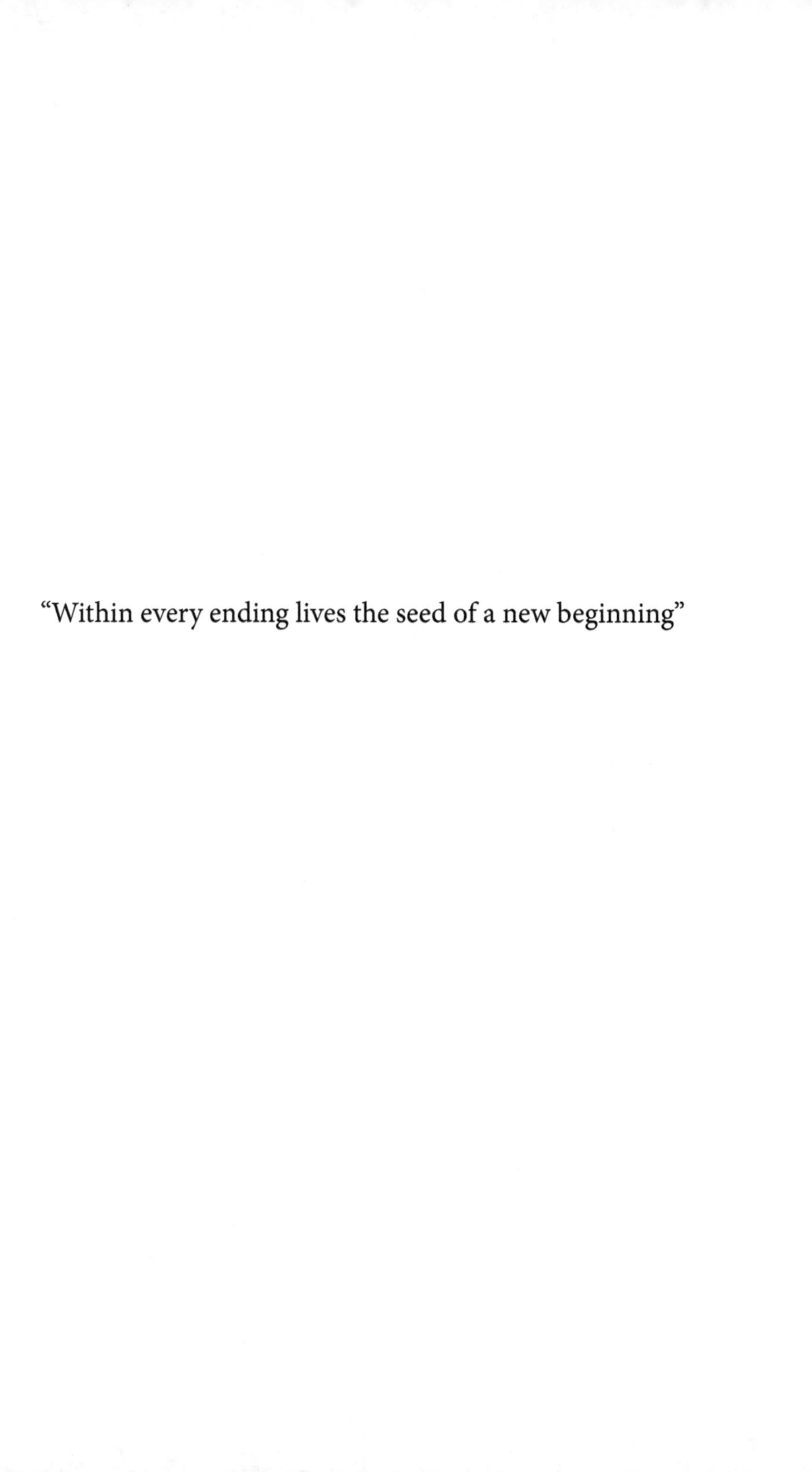

"Within every ending lives the seed of a new beginning"

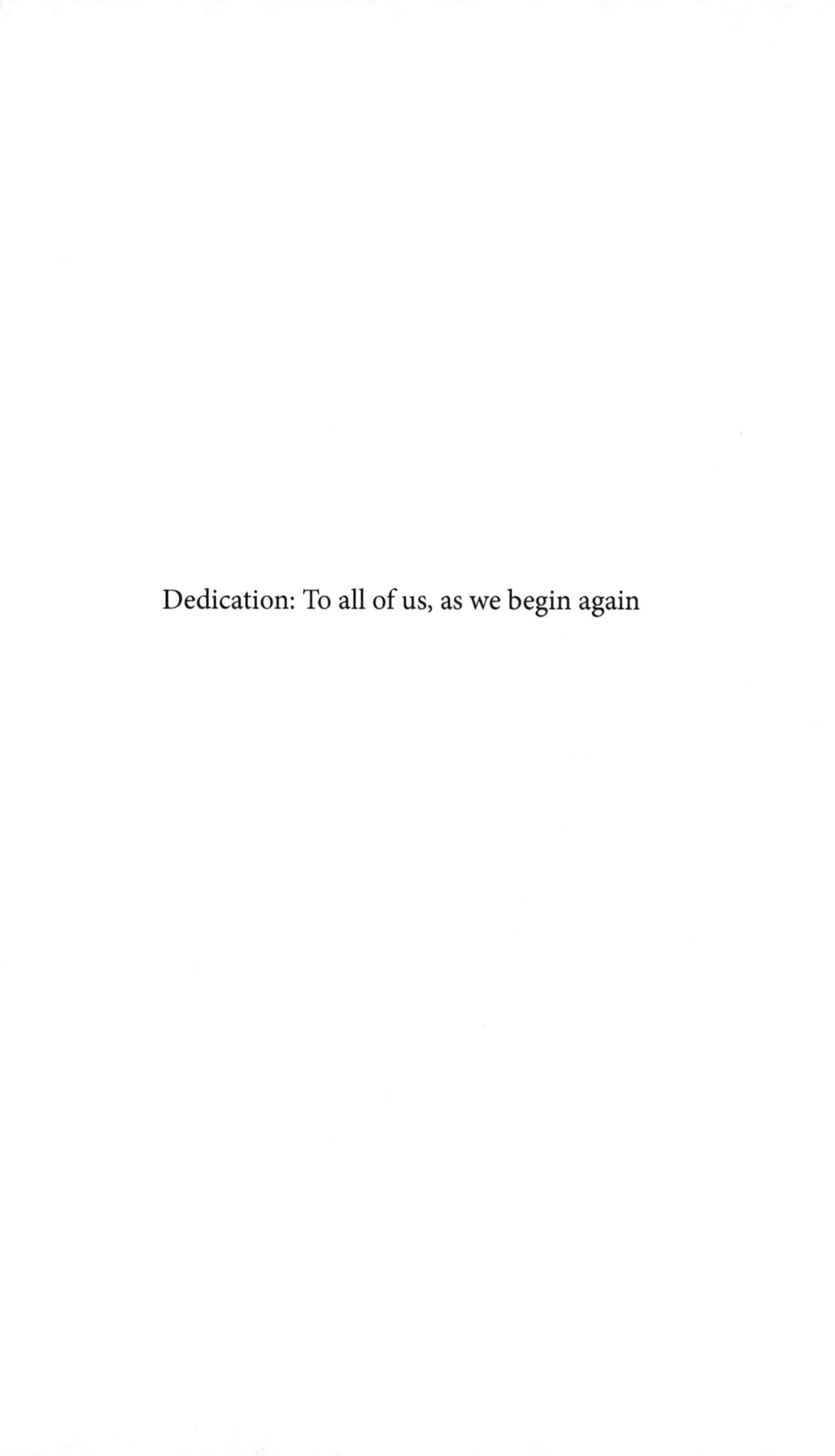

Dedication: To all of us, as we begin again

Always remembering Chris . . .
December 25, 1988 – August 4, 2013
"I see you"

"Strength does not come from physical capacity, it comes from an indomitable will."

—Gandhi

OTHER BOOKS BY ANNE

Walking the Path of Grief
Like a Rose
When Time Stands Still
In the Same Boat
Just Thinking
Sitting with the Mountain and a Dog Named Bear
Beginning Again…
Opening Doors
Stepping Stones
Always Beginning Again…
Reaching for the Light
Finding a New Way Home…
Letting Go…Holding On
Sometimes…You Just Breathe
Sometimes…You Just Watch and Wait
Sometimes…We Fall Slowly
Sometimes…We Rise Slowly

Contents

There Is Stillness

Last night
A storm blew through the area
There had been a strange stillness
And then out of nowhere it seemed
The wind picked up
The skies turned dark
The wind kept blowing
Branches broke
Power went out
Thunder – lightning
And then the rain
And after the rain
The quiet, the stillness returned…
Emotions are like that sometimes
There can be a stillness within
And then uneasiness
Your mood darkens
The questions, the guilt, the shame
Your heart hurts
You cry out, you sob
Unable to keep the pain inside
And then the tears flow
And after the tears
Gradually
There is quiet again
There is stillness once more

To Be like a Tree

To be like a tree
It seems
Would be to be strong and steady
To have a core that never moves
Rooted in truth
And yet
Flexible
Able to move with the wind
Bend in the storms
Protecting what is yours to protect
Always changing with the seasons
Growing
Always growing
Giving new life
Always giving new life

Destiny and Choice

His wife had just died
And he said
"No one chooses his destiny"
And I wondered
What he meant
And I wondered
Was he right?
Or could it be
That we do choose our destiny
Or maybe
It is our responses
To what happens to us
That create the path
To our destiny
And it is up to us
To make choices
To take that path
Or perhaps
Choose another

Christine

She died the other day
But not before writing
A heartfelt goodbye
What strength
What grace
To leave a love letter
For those who loved her
Leaving her best goodbye
Her best life advice
To never miss an opportunity to make someone's day
To do your best, try your hardest, kick some ass
To add to your happy
And in the end
To add to everyone's happy
To touch
And to be touched
To love
And to be loved

To See

To really see
You have to step back a little
Let your mind be quiet
And just watch and wait
And listen
And then you can see
Really see
And it will break your heart sometimes
To see
The harm done without knowing
The hurt that is right in front of us
And yet goes unacknowledged
The heartache
The missed step
And yes
To see
You may even need to close your eyes
And breathe
Just breathe
And let what is right in front of you
Be seen

Not Letting Go

I've come to believe
That you can't let go
Not really
You can rearrange
You can change where things fit
Or don't
We hold on to memories
And maybe that's
Where everything goes
Everything that we can't let go
They can become a memory
That we hold on to
And maybe the memory changes
Or even heals
Or is healed
But it's
Still there
Still a part of us
Informing our thoughts
Informing our choices
Making us who we are

Be a Friend

Sometimes
It's a struggle to take care of yourself
The idea of self-care
Seems indulgent somehow
But
It seems easier
To treat yourself as a friend
To think of yourself as a friend
Just that
Be a friend
To yourself
It could make all the difference

Changing Everything

Sometimes
It's good to decide
Who you want to be
How you want to be in this world
And then do it
Become who you want to be
Doing what you love
Just being yourself
And allowing others to be themselves
What a gift
For you
And for others
A gift that will heal
A gift that gives back
A gift that shines a light
And maybe
Changes everything
For everyone

Becoming Yourself

I read the words
"Let yourself evolve"
And they moved me deeply
To think about
Where I've been
Where I am
What my dreams once were
How I lost some dreams
And yet…
And yet
There are still dreams
Hopes and wishes
And it's okay
To take one step at a time
To keep moving forward
And become
Who you might be now
Now that there has been loss and pain
There can still be growth
There can still be changing
You can still evolve
You can still become
Yourself

Another Way

It is said
We never know
What life holds for us
And there is no truer truth
That we can plan
And we can try
Really hard
We can dream and wish and hope
We can do everything right
We can do everything wrong
And
Still
We never know
What life holds for us
There are always curveballs
There are always forks in the road
There are always blocks
There are always openings
There are always disappointments and heartaches
And there are surprises
And new beginnings
And whatever life does hold for us
There will always be
Another way to go

Choices

A wise woman once told me
With some life choices
There is nothing to lose
There is only the possibility
Of something
So maybe
Sometimes
The thing to do
Is to be brave
And do the thing
That frightens you
The thing outside your comfort zone
"Just do it"
And follow where it takes you
And maybe
The choice you make
Will take you to possibilities
And there will be something
To hold on to

Possibilities

When you reach for possibilities
You also let go
Let go of what no longer exists
At least
Not the way it was
It ended
Perhaps suddenly
Perhaps slowly
But it is no more
And the only way to heal
To really heal
Is to let go
Reach for what may be
Reach for what could be
Reach for possibilities

Something Beautiful

It is said
You can build something beautiful
From what is broken
And it takes
Being vulnerable
Being transparent
Being open
With others
Who can see and hear
Who can be vulnerable
And transparent and open
Because, then
You can hold each other up
You can hold faith and hope
For each other
You can be
Something beautiful
You can be
A light in the darkness
Something beautiful
From what is broken

Reminding Myself

Walking alone
Sometimes
Can feel like being broken
But
It is said
Something beautiful
Can come from what is broken
So
Go for a walk
Get lost
And
Be found
Put your phone away sometimes
So you can be in the present
So you can see and hear what is really there
Slow down a bit
So that squirrel running by
Or chipmunk or raccoon or deer
Can live to see another day
Take pictures
Draw something
Write a letter
Sing a song
Forgive
Plant a flower
Give someone a hug

Love the one you are with
Appreciate what you have
Be kind
Give grace
Be gentle
Make plans
And allow for serendipity
Hold the light for someone
For everyone
Remember what's important to you
And to others
Be mindful in everything you do
Giving it meaning
Knowing it matters
Knowing time is precious
Knowing how beautiful life is
Breathing in
Breathing out
Walking alone
Walking beside someone
Someone who needs
Reminding perhaps
There is always beauty
That can come from what is broken

It's Not Your Fault

Sometimes
When you hit the proverbial wall
When grief is so overwhelming
When you are drowning in your own tears
You need to be reminded
It's not your fault
People make choices
Or, at least, for whatever reasons
Make decisions
Do things
That are not good for them
May be harmful to them
Even to the point of death
Sometimes
There are just tragic accidents
Poor judgment calls
Circumstances beyond our control
And
In order to heal
You really need to hear
It's not your fault
You really need to see
It's not your fault
You really need to believe
It's not your fault
It's really
Not your fault

Permission

Sometimes
The greatest gift
You can give another
Is permission
Permission to speak
To speak their truth
To say something is not working
To say what they need
To acknowledge what is important to them
To ask what is possible…or not
And then
Permission to stay
Or
When it's time
Permission to leave
And
Sometimes
That is the greatest gift you can give yourself
Permission
Permission to speak your truth
Permission to stay
Or
When it's time
Permission to leave

On Being Mindful

Doing something mindfully
No matter what it is
Whether it is
Creating something
Fixing something
Cleaning the something
Holding someone's hand
Writing a poem
Traveling
Planting a tree
Tending the garden
Rescuing a dog or cat, bird or spider
Walking your dog
Or someone else's
You name it
Doing everything
Doing nothing
Doing it mindfully
Gives it meaning
And when it has meaning
It matters
The way you do it matters
When you take your time
Stay in the present
Time feels precious
And there is gratitude

And when there is gratitude
There can be joy
Flowing into what you are doing
Or not doing
Everything becomes precious
Nothing is wasted
Especially your time
Time is not wasted
And there is a feeling
A sense of being
Being where you are meant to be
Doing what you are meant to do

Just Listen

It is said
That feelings are there for a reason
And, so
When you are aware
Of a feeling
Maybe the best thing to do
To learn, to change, to grow
Is to ask that feeling
What is it trying to teach you
And, then
Listen
Just listen
Breathe
Just breathe
And let the feeling
Show you
What it is there to teach
Show you
What you need to learn

To Let Go

Healing is a curious thing
You think your world has come to an end
And to carry on
The answer it is said
Is to let go
And that
Feels like it would be the end of you
And maybe
In a way it is
But
When you let go
It is not the end
It is a beginning
It is full of possibilities
In part
Because
You are a different person
You look through a different lens
And your world looks different
Through the lens of loss
Through the lens of letting go

What's Right

To know what is right
At least, for you
You sometimes have to realize
What is wrong
So that
Sometimes
You have to do things
Undo things
Try things
Let things go
Be with someone
Be without someone
Sometimes
You have to learn something
Feel something
Before you know
If it's right for you
Or not

Some Things

It is true what is said
About some things
That
You don't heal from some things
But
There can still be new beginnings
When you turn around
Take a deep breath
Dust yourself off
And keep going
One step at a time
One breath at a time
To live your life
In spite of some things
That
Just don't heal

This Journey

There are times on this journey called life
That we fall
Finding ourselves on the ground
Sometimes wondering how we got there
And then, perhaps
Realizing
You're still on a journey
And the next step
Is to rise up
Stand up
And keep going
Because
After all
Falling and getting up again
Are both
Part of this journey
Called life

The One Healing Story

We all seem to be living
Two stories
Or
At least between two stories
The outward story
The one that anyone can see
And then there is the inner story
The one that we tell ourselves
The one we share sometimes
But not always
Because
Maybe it feels too vulnerable
Too personal
Too revealing
But, what if
We were to share our inner stories more often
And found our inner stories
To have things in common
Or, at least some similarities
Maybe, we could stop living between the stories
We could build connections, bridges
We could be okay with silence
With listening
We could see each other
Really see each other
We could hear each other

Really hear each other
We could know
That every life matters
And we could live just one story
The one healing story

A Different Question

It's easy, sometimes
To get on a kind of thought treadmill
Asking the same questions
Getting the same answers
That lead back to the same questions
So
Maybe
The answer is
To ask a different question
Step off the "treadmill"
Find out
What it really is
That you want to know
Find out
What it really is
That will bring you peace

Feelings

The hard truth
About feelings
Is
They may be real
They are valid
But
They aren't always
Based in reality
They aren't always
Real
We may feel afraid
When there is nothing to be afraid of
We may feel discouraged
When
We're really just learning
We may feel less than
When it's just a story we tell ourselves
So maybe
The thing to do
With difficult feelings
Is make sure they are real
And then
Feel what you need to feel

Healing

Healing is a process
A pilgrimage
A passage
A journey
And so
It's important to allow the journey
To allow the time
Whatever time it takes
To step into the journey
To wander
To find one's way
To make one's way
To breathe into
To heal into
Who you want to be

On Cocooning

I've heard people saying lately
That they are cocooning
Meaning they are going within
Meaning its too tough and scary out in the world
Meaning they are needing to be protected
The cocoon, though
Is a dark place
A temporary place to go
A quiet place
A place to process what is troubling
A place to find yourself, your voice, your truth
A place to process grief
A place to watch and wait
Until you overcome your fear
Until you are feeling strong enough again
And when you are ready
When you have the courage again
To open
To begin again
To find the light
To find your way
That is when you will come back into the world again
Ready to carry on
Ready to offer what you have
With love, with hope, with peace in your heart
Ready to come back to life
Ready to go forward once more
Ready to be the change

Love What You Love

I read something recently
About not holding back
From your own love and life
And I thought
What a good thing
To aspire to
Just love what you love
No holding back
No shame
No regrets
Just love your life
It's the only one you get
As far as we know
So love your life
Know you are just where you are meant to be
Being who you're meant to be
Know you are here for a reason
For a purpose
Know that you matter
Just as you are
Even when things are falling apart
Even as you learn and grow and change

Note to Self

It is said
That facts come from outside
And truth comes from inside
So, maybe
The next time you are making a harsh judgment
You could catch yourself
Ask yourself
Is it true
Are you being compassionate
Are you being kind
Ask yourself again
Is it true
Chances are
You could reframe your thoughts
You could find a different response
See the truth
Know the truth
Be with the truth
The truth that comes from inside

The Feeling of Home

I wonder sometimes
What is the feeling of home
Maybe it is different for different people
And maybe
Probably
Some things are the same
Warmth…
Coziness…
Acceptance…
Hope…
Contentment…
Safety…
Peace…
Familiar things…
Memories…
Gentle hugs…
The feeling of home
Something of the heart
Something in the heart
And maybe
To find the feeling of home
You have to be home
With yourself
Be home
With who you are
And know
You are always home

Waiting

Waiting can be a totally different experience
Depending on what you're waiting for
Waiting for a baby's first breath
Waiting for a loved one's last breath
Waiting for the test results
Waiting to hear if you got the job, the house, the prize
But all this waiting
It's all filled with anticipation
And a sense of standing in place
Not being able to move on
Whether it will be with joy
Or with heartbreak
While you wait
Time will stand still
And it can still be a time filled with wonder
The wonder of beginnings
The wonder of endings
The wonder of life

Watching

I've been reminded lately
When watching others navigate life and death
As difficult and challenging as it may be
The only answer to their questions
Is to meet them where they are
To hold my breath perhaps
Come up for air when I need to
But
To love them
Support them on their journey
It's okay
To bless their journey
Even if they can't see what is true
Keep watching and waiting with them
Don't turn away
But stay
Give them space
Offer them a safe place
To do life
And death
On their terms

Winter Day Dreams

I saw a sign the other day
It said "Let's stay Home"
And being the homebody I am
I had to buy it
So now, it sits on my shelf
Between the "believe" sign
And the "Home" sign
And it invites me
To a winter day of dreams
And, so
I go down memory lane
Even bringing out the family photos
Grateful for the memories
Grateful for the times away
Grateful for the dreams
And all the adventures
And grateful for the times
We just stayed home

Grateful Tears

Sometimes
When you are healing
The tears that fall
Seem to change
They start to feel different somehow
They fall more softly, more quietly
More gently
And as the darkness
Turns into light
The tears
Become grateful tears
Tears filled with gratitude
Gratitude for the memories
For the stories
For the strength and resilience
For the love and support
For life
Not the life that you imagined
But just gratitude
For life

Cultivating Gratitude

I love the idea of wandering
And wondering
It encourages staying in the present moment
Being mindful
Cultivating gratitude
There is a calmness
A peacefulness
When wandering
And wondering
And I want to see my life
Through the lens of wonder and gratitude
And so
I wander
And I wonder
Living an ordinary life
Slowing down
As I walk the dog
Stopping to say hi to the deer and the other creatures
Scurrying by
Admiring the rocks
Slowing down
To brush the cat
Make tea, bake cookies
To read and write, to take pictures
To walk to the mailbox
Slowing down

To spend time with friends and family
To reflect, to light candles
To watch the sun rise and set, the moon, the stars
Wandering
Wondering
Cultivating gratitude

Just Once More

In the deep of winter
And sometimes
Well, anytime
There comes the thought
Just once more
If only
We could see him
Hear him
Feel him
Be with him
Just once more
Look into those eyes
Feel his warmth
See that wonderful smile
Touch him
Just once more
Hug him
Be hugged by him
Hold his hand
Love him
Just once more, but then
Comes the thought
Just once more
Would never be enough

Beautiful Moments

There are such beautiful moments
On this journey we call life
A baby's first breath
The feel of skin on skin
When you are seen and heard
When you see and hear another
When you hear the words "I love you"
And even better
You feel them
And speak them
Such beautiful moments
Watching the sun rise or set
Sitting by the fire
Remembering
Telling stories
Laughing
And, of course
S'mores
A cool breeze on your cheeks
A quiet walk in the woods
An afternoon alone with a book
An evening with your family laughing
Such beautiful moments
On the journey we call life
We need nothing more
Just some beautiful moments to remember
To cherish
To hold on to

Leaning into Hope

It's hard sometimes
To lean into hope
When life becomes full of challenges
But, then again
The stars shine brightest
In the darkness
The rainbow glows
After the storm
The sky is bluest
When the clouds move on
Flowers bloom
After the winters cold
And
It only takes
A little love
A little hug
A thoughtful gesture
To make a difference
So, yes
Whenever life's challenges
Knock on your door
Lean
Lean into hope

Alone

Being human
Sometimes, we feel alone
And
Being human
Is how we know we are not alone
Being human
Reminds us we are not alone in our struggles
Even
When we feel very alone
If we reach out
Someone usually reaches back
Reminding us
Of the value of others
Of the value of ourselves
So, know you are not alone
Reach out
Or reach back
Be human

To Be Here Now

I used to think
To believe at some level
That in order to be with life
To really live in the present
The pain needs to be healed
To be gone
But now
I realize
Some of the pain will never be gone
It is a part of me now
It rests within me
Sometimes coming to the surface
But more and more
Resting in the depths of me
And from there
It can add to my depth, perhaps
It can guide me in my life
So that
In fact
I am more with life than ever
Living in the present
Being reminded
All the time
To be here now

The One Question

I came across a question the other day
One that will not let go
Maybe because
It is one question
That has an answer
When other questions so often
Have no answers
"What does healing ask of us?"
It asks us to start where we are
It asks us to show up again and again and again
It asks us to begin again
Every day
That's all
Just begin again
And really
That is what life asks of us too
To just begin again

Allowing Experience to Teach Us

What is the truth of our lives?
Is it waking up
Is it seeing what is in front of us
Or, behind us
Is it acceptance
Is it holding on
Or letting go
Maybe
It is all of that
Seeing our experiences for what they are
Allowing them to teach us
To nurture us
To help us grow
To help us hold on
And to let go

Letting the Past Be

To let the past be
Is to accept life as it was
And as it is
Is to accept you cannot change what has been
To know it is unchangeable
While at the same time
Forgiving the other
Forgiving yourself
For what you saw
For what you knew
For what you could have stopped
Forgiving the other
Forgiving yourself
For what you couldn't see
For what you couldn't know
For what you couldn't stop
Forgiving the other
Forgiving yourself

What We Hold

There are some things
That sometimes
We cannot "get over"
We never "get over"
But
We can be with it
We can know
Nothing is going to change
Except, if we allow it
The way we hold it can change
So that
Life can go on
Life does go on
We can find our way
Even
When we don't
When we can't
"Get over" the something
That we have to hold on to

Your Life

I read the other day
"Your life belongs to you"
And I wondered
Is that true
Because sometimes
Someone else's life
Hijacks yours
Because they have died
And left you bereft
Or they have made bad choices
And left you crushed
But then again
If I believe
My life belongs to me
Then
I am responsible for my growth
I am accountable for my choices
And so
Yes
My life belongs to me

Signs

On this journey called life
There may not be a map
But
There are signs along the way
Getting stuck
Going too fast
Going too slow
Feeling lost
Going around in circles
Finding yourself in the dark
Being late all the time
Being frustrated all the time
Being at a standstill
Doing the same things
Over and over again
While telling yourself
You'll do better tomorrow
All signs
That something needs to change
All signs
It's time
To find another way

To Nurture Things

It seems
That life always comes back
To beginning again
We must always be willing
To begin again
And just as in nature
We can't force things
But
We can
Nurture things
Nurture new beginnings
Nurture the things
That will help our life grow
Will help us to create
The life
That belongs to us
The life
That is ours to grow

Because of Them

There comes a time
Sometimes
When you begin
To fill the hole left by another
You begin to hold something new
New life
With light and love
With peace
With old and new memories
With the things you love
With happiness
And though these things
Will not replace the one you lost
They will be held
By the hole they left
By the opening they left
Will be held surrounded by their love, their hopes and dreams
Will be there sometimes
Because of them
Will be more precious, perhaps
Because of them

Trust the Journey

I've been thinking, a lot, lately
About why I'm here
And, of course
We each have to find the answer to that question for ourselves
But
It does seem
That one thing for all of us to learn
Is to trust the journey
No matter what
Trust the journey
For there will be signs
There are always signs
Assurances perhaps
That you are going the right way
Or
That it is time to turn around
To begin again
And
To still
Trust the journey

Grace in Darkness

It may not feel like it
When you are in a dark place
But there is grace in darkness
There is stillness
There are memories that whisper
Whispering of times gone by
Reminders of love and light
Of smiles and laughter
Of someone looking over their shoulder at you
Of hugs and holding hands
Of warmth
Of secrets shared
A kiss on your cheek
A gentle touch
Grace in darkness
Stillness
Whispers

To Die Well

To die well
It is said
Is
To have lived well
Is
To have loved
And been loved
To have learned and grown and changed
To have known
And to have not known
To have gone with the flow
To have watched
To have waited
To have healed
To have gotten into some good trouble
To have done what was needed
When it was needed
How it was needed
To have known "it is now"
To have understood that everyone suffers
To have wept
To have laughed
To have been lost and been found
To have wandered
And wondered
At the beauty
And the brokenness
Of this amazing life

Just Watching

Walking on the beach
There are so many wonders of this life to find
Just listening to the waves and the wind
Feeling the warmth of the sun
The coldness of the water
Just watching wonders of this life
People walking by
Running by
Jogging by
People walking their dogs
People setting up their umbrellas
People riding bikes
Tossing footballs
Laughing
Crying
Just standing, watching, waiting
Looking out at the waves, the sun, the wonders of this life
People on cell phones
On iPads
Talking
Singing
Listening
Just watching some wonders of this life
And thinking what a wonderful world we have

Do That…Always

It is said
No matter what the question is
The simplest answer
Is love
Always
And in this moment
When there is so much fear
Confusion, cruelty
Angst and uncertainty
No matter what the question is
The simplest…the only answer
Is love
Always
And the question
What would love do
In this moment
Has only one answer
To simply
Love
Do that
Always

More Than One Ending

There are times in our lives
When it is important
Imperative
That we speak our truth
And if all around us are silent
To speak our truth
Could be the difference
Could give others the strength
The courage
To speak their truth
So when you can
Be brave
Speak to the noise
Speak to the silence
For there is more than one story
There is always more than one story
And more than one ending

The Privilege to Live

I sat down the other day
To spend time with an elderly woman
She shared some stories of her life
I asked her, at the end of her sharing
What was it like
For her
Knowing she was approaching the end of her life
She paused for a moment
And then she said
It has been a wonderful life
And I think
What a privilege
To have had the chance
To live
To love
To be here
So I am not afraid
I am just grateful
Grateful to have had this chance
To have had this life
To have had this privilege

Becoming

It is said
We are always becoming
Everything is a process
Of learning and growing and changing
Of becoming
For tomorrow brings new possibilities
New lessons
New understandings
Time for healing
Time for opening the heart and mind
Time for becoming

Finding Peace

The things that scare us
Are there for a reason
Are there to teach us something
And facing whatever scares us
Being with the fear
And doing it anyway
Healing what is causing it
This is the way to growing
This is the way to changing
To becoming who you are meant to be
To being fully yourself
To taking your life by storm
Lightning and thunder included
And then the quiet
And the peace that follows

The Need Is More Healing

It is said
If you are trying to do something
And it's just not happening
Whether it is getting healthier
Stronger
Happier
Whether it is getting more accomplished
Getting more focused
More consistent
Whether it is getting more patient
More loving
More caring
Then what you need
Is not more motivation
More commitment
More wanting
But rather
What you need
Is more healing
What you need
Is more healing…

To Be

To feel connected
Is to feel accepted
And to feel accepted
Is to feel loved
To feel wanted
To feel like a piece of the puzzle
A loop in the chain
To belong
And to belong
Is to feel at home
Is to feel safe
Is to feel
Is to feel connected
Is to be

About Healing

It is said
Healing
Is never as close as we hope
Or
As far as we fear
It is one breath at a time
One step at a time
It is
Watching for the signs
Following the signs
Signs that tell us which way to go
It is doing that
It is the journey
Being between the signs
Staying the course
Being in the present
Noticing what remains
It is
Coming to a place of gratitude
And
Practicing that
Just practicing that

Heart to Heart

There is a power in warmth
The warmth of the heart
Of connection
Of gentleness
Of kindness
Of taking care
Of seeing
Really seeing
Who we are
Where we are
How we are
The warmth of understanding
Of recognizing how we are the same in so many ways
How we need closeness, compassion, bridges
We need bridges
Not walls
Not barriers
But bridges
We need bridges
Coming from the heart
Connecting
Heart to heart

In Between

Sometimes
Maybe, most of the time
It feels like I'm "in between"
Never quite becoming
Never quite knowing
Who I am
What I'm meant to do
Why I'm here
Not wanting to leave
Not knowing where to go
Belonging only with those
Who are leaving
And how can you belong
With the ones who are leaving
Always saying goodbye
Always needing more time
Needing rest, softness, peace
And maybe
That's why I stay in the "in between"
That's where I can take a deep breath
That's where I can rest
Be soft
Find peace

The In-Between

We often live
In the "in-between" places
When something has ended
And a new beginning has not yet come to be
And so
We must wait
In the in-between
Wait for healing
Wait for guidance
Wait for love
Wait for new beginnings
But, oh
To open the heart, mind, and soul
To the in-between
Where the magic of growth
And transformation lives
Where the magic of possibility
Of grace
Of beginning again
Waits
Where the magic lives

To Keep Healing

It's important to care
It's always important to care
But sometimes
It's important
To clear your own energy
To let yourself be free
So that you don't stop caring
So that
You don't get "burned out"
So care
Always care
But, don't forget
To put it down
Give yourself time and space
To keep becoming
To keep healing

Holding Hope for Healing

Sometimes
You need fierce love
A love that is kind
A love that is compassionate
A love that can imagine the possibilities
Sometimes
You need a love that holds hope
That holds you
That just stays close
Stands by you
Sits quietly with you
Breathes with you
Sometimes
You need a love that stays on the journey with you
Hears you
Sees you
Understands the darkness
A love that holds the light
Sometimes
You need a love that surrounds you
That keeps you safe
A love that is strong for you
A love that prays and sings
A love that sometimes screams and cries
A love that smiles through the tears
A love that holds the faith for you

A love that brings you back home
Back to peace
Sometimes
You need a fierce love

That's All

Sometimes
It feels like there is nothing we can do
It feels like the mountain is too high
The road is too long
The way is too hard
The obstacles too big
The pain, the fear too deep
It is then
That we are called to do the next right thing
It doesn't have to be big
Just a small thing
And then another small thing
Another right thing
Sometimes
That is the only thing to do
One step
One breath
Staying grounded
Doing one right thing
One small, right thing
That's all
Just keep doing that

Everything Changes

Watching the dark clouds roll by
Listening to the thunder
Seeing the rain falling
And the flashes of lightning
I am reminded
That no one stays the same
No one is one way or another
We change
Just like the weather
The sun will come out
The air will become still
Or
There may be a soft breeze
And then harsh winds
It will be hot
It will be cold
It will be clear
It will be foggy
Everything changes
Our emotions change
We must remember that
Our emotions change
Again and again and again

Life Changes Us

As I look out of the window
This gray, rainy day
I cannot really see
What is clearly seen on a sunny day
The water
The trees and houses across the lake
Spots of green are visible
From the bushes by the windows
But beyond that, gray
Just gray
Until the clouds begin to shift
The grayness lifts
The light returns
And my vision becomes more clear
The trees and houses in the distance return
And it reminds me
Of how life changes us
How we grow and change
How we can go down rabbit holes
How our vision can be blurry
How we can begin to see more clearly
How we can be here now
Changing
Always changing

Taking a Deep Breath

I was reminded the other day
That you can be sitting next to someone
You can be in the same room with others
And yet
You can be miles away
Having a completely different experience
For your mind may wander
Your heart may be somewhere else
Completely somewhere else
Lost in a memory
Struggling to breathe
Trying once more
To make sense of it
And then maybe
You feel a gentle touch
Someone's hand on your back
You hear a quiet voice
Calling you back
Back to the present
And you come back
A little unsteady
But grateful to be taking a deep breath
Grateful to be back in the room

Communion

I've been thinking lately
About the idea of loving with open hands
And I realize
That's not so easy to do
To open your hands and heart
Whether to give
Or to receive
But to open your hands
To receive
Seems harder somehow
It makes you vulnerable
It may make you feel needy
Maybe you are needy
You may open your hands in a gentle way
Receiving bread and wine for what it is
Or for what it might be
Trusting there is love
You may open your hands
In a desperate way
Maybe you are hungry or weary or broken
Maybe you need food or shelter or warmth
Maybe you need reassurance, truth, or rest
Maybe you need connection, or love, or to feel you belong
But
Whether it is in a gentle way or a desperate way
If you open your hands

If you receive the bread and the wine
For what it is
Or for what it might be
It is a promise
A promise of life
A promise to hold on
For one more day
Just by opening your hands
It is a promise
To wait
To stay
It is a promise
To trust
To trust there is love

The Heart Knows

There is an ache in the heart
It seems
A place
Where the heart knows
The love you have lost
And the love you will lose someday
A place
Where the memories are
A place that knows
How precious each day is
Each moment
And when you visit that place
You find it is not a place to run from
It may take you to your knees sometimes
It may warm your heart sometimes
May even make you smile
You find it is a place for gratitude
A place where love grows
Where you find
So many precious memories
Just like those time-hop photos
Where you see the wonder and the impermanence of life
The beauty, the sadness
The triumphs and the tragedies
All happening together
Always happening together

And you see
Life goes on
Life always goes on

To Turn Around

Sometimes
It takes a while
To turn around
To let go
To begin again
But when you do let go
So very often
That is when you begin again
The clouds begin to clear
You begin to breathe more softly
Your heart fills with gratitude
For what was
Not so much for what was lost
But for what you had
And for what is
When you turn around
And see
In the gentle light
You are just where you need to be
Coming home
Surrounded by love, hope, and peace
Sometimes
It just takes a while to turn around

To Just Be

Summer is coming to an end
And with that ending
There comes a feeling of melancholy
An undefined sadness
Something that gives me pause
And I sigh
I slip into not knowing
And so
I wonder
What is this feeling here to teach me
This melancholy
This sadness
This not knowing
That something is shifting perhaps
The breeze is changing direction
And I
I too am changing direction
Moving toward home
Leaning into the quiet
Becoming
Letting myself be
Just be
And letting that be enough

The Beginning Again

It is said
That letting go is not the end
It is the beginning
And maybe that is true
When you come to the knowing
To the understanding
That in reality
When you open your heart and hands
To let go
You also open your heart and hands
To receive, to hold on
To carry on
To carry what is left with care and gentleness
To hold on
To the love, the memories, the connections
The smiles, the laughter
And yes, the tears
You hold on to gratitude
And gratitude grows
Wraps its arms around you
Holds you
Comforts you
Changes you
Walks with you as you begin again

To Change Your Story

Sometimes
There are
Parts of your story
You want to change
Sometimes
Are desperate to change
Because
Sometimes
It feels like too much
To think the thoughts
To picture what happened
To say the words
To feel the pain
To try to explain
And, so
Sometimes
The only thing to do
To change the story
Is to say
Over and over and over again
You are forgiven, you are forgiven, you are forgiven
To give yourself
To give him
To give her
The gift of saying
The gift of believing
You couldn't have known

That Will Be Enough

I've heard it said
That nothing can change
Until it is faced
And
That it is also true
That not everything that is faced
Can be changed
And, those are the things
Maybe
You have to change the way you hold them
The way you interpret them
The way you translate their meaning
So that
You don't carry what is not yours to carry
You don't grieve what is not yours to grieve
You don't compare what you have to give
You just know
You carry what you can
You grieve what you must
You give what you have to give
And that
That will be enough

What We Remember

We don't always get to choose
What happens to us
And
There are some questions
That have no answers
Some things
That leave us forever asking why
No answer will ever fix those things
No answer will ever be enough
But
We do get to choose
How those things shape us
How they grow us
Who we become
What good we keep
What good we remember
Let the good
Be what we remember

Just Stay

There is a Rumi quote
"Out beyond ideas of right doing and wrong doing
There is a field.
I will meet you there"
It feels like
Right now
Before we all become stories
Of what could have been
What should have been
We could meet
Out there
In the beyond
To connect
To see each other
To hear each other
To agree
Even to disagree
But to stay
Stay together
Be present
Hold each other
Support each other
To not fight
Or if we do fight
To not leave
To not go away

Just stay
Stay in the story
The one about coming together
The one about growing love
The one about growing peace

The Wisdom of Nature

I find myself wanting to listen to the wisdom of nature
To the wisdom of the trees
The trees with their deep roots
Roots that reach out to each other
Holding on to each other
Giving each other strength
Strength to stand during the storms of life
And at the same time
Their branches sway in the wind
Staying connected
But not entangled
And
When it's time
The trees
They let go gently
Their leaves surrendering softly
Falling to the earth below
Nurturing that same earth
And when a tree has lived its life
It falls into the arms of Mother Earth
Still giving itself to the cycles of life
Giving itself to life
Giving itself
To life

Seeds

It is said
Our thoughts are the seeds that grow us
We become what we think about
We become what we practice
And I wonder at what I think about
About what I practice
I want to believe in love
I want to believe in peace
I want to heal
I want to trust, to have faith
I want to be good enough
But sometimes
Love and peace are lost
Healing is not possible
Trust is broken
Faith is uncertain
Being good is not enough
And so
Sometimes
Our thoughts
Our beliefs
Are always just seeds
They don't grow
They can't grow
They just wait
And sometimes

Maybe
That is enough
It might even be growing a seed
To just wonder
What you are thinking about right now
So ask yourself
What are you thinking about?
What are you thinking about
Right now?

To Collect Quotes

Sometimes
I think I must not have very deep roots
The kind that keep you grounded
The kind that help you grow
And so
I became a "collector of quotes"
Quotes that guide my steps, my thoughts
Quotes that support my hopes and dreams
Quotes that keep me from withering
Quotes that give me a compass
So that
I can find a way to live with intention
I can find my way
As if I had deep roots
As if I were grounded
As if I believed in the quotes
I have collected
The quotes
I have even tattooed on my arms
So they have become a part of me
A part of me who is grounded
A part of me who is still growing and hoping and dreaming

Doorways

I've always loved doorways
As if there's something magical behind a closed door
But
They usually remind me of the leaving
When someone says goodbye
And walks away
Sometimes you find a door that opens
You find yourself going down memory lane
Maybe reading letters or looking at photos
Maybe just remembering
You let your heart lead the way
And then it's not the leaving that matters
But the coming back
You find your way back
Finally realizing
That this is where you belong
At this doorway
The one that opens
And as you step inside
Your heart opens
Your heart says
Welcome home
And all you need to do
At this doorway
Is to let your heart lead the way
Let your heart be your teacher
Let your heart open

Purpose

To find our purpose
Is to find our anchor
Is to find our why
And our how
And to find our purpose, a purpose to carry on
In the midst of grief
Is to find our light in the darkness
Is to find our lifesaver in the waves
Is to find a way to breathe
When there is no more air
Is to find a way to go forward
When life has turned upside down

On Not Figuring Things Out

I am just learning
After all this time
After all the ups and downs
After all the trying to make sense of life
All the trying to understand
The trying to figure things out
We don't actually have to have figured it out
To live an authentic life
Rooted in love and kindness
It doesn't require a certain belief
It's more about a way of moving through the world
It's about telling the truth about you
Not pretending
Asking questions is okay
And just choosing love
Always
Active love
Fierce love
Compassionate love
Trusting that kindness — even when quiet and unseen
It changes things

Gratitude

It is said
That gratitude
Brings you to the present
Keeps you in the present
Reminds you to be here now
Because
Your heart is in it
Because
You remember
All time
Is quality time
Just because it is all you have
Time
And no matter what you are doing
Somehow
It is
Quality time
So don't forget
Put your heart in it
Be grateful
And you will be here now

When There Is an End

Sometimes
The way is hard to find
Even when you are on the way
And so
Sometimes
It helps to let your heart lead the way
It helps to know love is often quiet
And it helps
To know
Life is more beautiful
Because
There is an end to the story
There is meaning
There is purpose
Because there is an end to the story

To Hold Both

I was walking my dog in the woods the other day
Having had a rough morning
When the tears of grief and loss visited once more
And it was a beautiful day though it was
Gray and cool and breezy
We approached another walker on the path
Trying to quickly pick up her dog
Saying "sometimes she growls…"
I smiled, walked a few more steps
Then turned and said
"Actually, sometimes I do too…"
The walker paused
And then she laughed
The most delightful, knowing laugh
That rang out through the woods
And I thought
There it is
Grief in one hand
Joy in the other
It is possible
It is okay
It is necessary
It is life-giving
To hold both

Who You Are Being

I've been wondering lately
Curious really
About what it means
When someone says
It's not who you are, it's who you are being
Who you are, it seems, is your identity, your labels
While who you are being, is how you move through the world
And through your life
How you show up
What story you tell
What path you take
And so
No matter who you are
You may be the one who lets others know
They are seen
They are heard
They matter
Because
Maybe
You are being the one who is present
You are being the one who is inspiring
You are being the one who brings calm and peace
The one who brings kindness and compassion
Maybe, you are being the one who brings laughter and lets others breathe

Maybe, you are being the one who brings mercy, love, forgiveness, or grace
You are being the one who brings responsibility, focus, or clarity
Maybe you are being the one who carries the truth
Maybe, you are being the one who holds the light
The one who gives words to the brokenhearted
Who brings calm to the anxious, courage to the fearful
Maybe, you are being the one who holds the pain and grief, the one who remembers
Maybe you are being the one who shows up
Who holds hope and faith
You are being the one on the path
You are being the one to show us
How we keep going
How we keep going
Together

Happiness and Tears

There is a saying
That
Happiness is on the other side
Of the tears
We have not shed
But when are the tears you have shed
Enough?
Sometimes
It feels like there is no end
To the tears
And no matter how much work you do
How much "healing" you do
How many tears you shed
There are more to come
But
Life goes on
There is gratitude
And love and times of peace
There is happiness
And so
I shed the tears that come
I hold some in my heart
And still
There is happiness, there is life

Floating

Sometimes
The work of healing is forever
And
Sometimes
When I need a break
From the pain
From the ache
From the exhaustion of it all
I imagine myself turning over in the water
After a long swim
And floating
Just floating
Sometimes with my eyes closed
Sometimes looking up at the sky
Watching the stars and the moon
Seeing the light in the darkness
Feeling the coolness of the water
The softness
Letting it hold me
Letting me rest

Tattoos

I got my first tattoo
When I turned fifty
A simple red rose
For I had always loved the rose
And the words of the song by the same name
And then, later
I got one that says
“Imagine being loved”
And then one that says
“I see you”
And then one that says
“Love is the anchor”
And another that says
“Never give up”
And these tattoos
As I imagine is true for others
Tell a story
And these tattoos of mine
They tell my story

Being Strong

I've been told
I am strong
Resilient
As if this is a prize
Something to be proud of
And I am grateful
That I have weathered the storms of my life
I've had the support and care I needed
The love to keep going
And yet
The other side
Of strength
Is often fragility
And there are times
I feel small
I feel broken
And not strong at all
But life goes on
I keep going
More so because of knowing
The fragility of life
Not so much
From being strong

One Step at a Time

Life
It seems
Is all about endings
Or preparing for endings
And then
Sometimes
Being in the in-between
And beginning again
And all of it
It seems
Is about
Learning to hold things gently, lightly
To let go in the in-between times
And keep taking one step at a time
To just keep walking
One step at a time

Life as a Storm

Someone asked me
What would it look like
If I took my life by storm?
And I thought
Maybe I would be less afraid
Maybe I would just
Be myself
While accepting others as they are
Maybe I would speak my truth
Find my voice
Maybe I would feel more peace, more joy
More compassion
Maybe I would love more deeply
Feel more completely
I would listen to that voice
The one that says
You do you
Be brave
Be strong
Keep going
And I would know
The calm
The calm that comes
When you take your life by storm

Beauty in the Darkness

It is said
That there is beauty within darkness
Beauty that is growth
And that is true in nature
The caterpillar in the cocoon
The seed in the dark earth
The roots in the ground
The tree in the acorn
The flower in the seed
The chick in the egg
The baby in the womb
All changing and growing
Changing and growing
Growing toward a new beginning
A new life
And so
It makes sense
That we too
Could be changing and growing
In our own dark places
Changing and growing
Growing toward new beginnings
Growing toward new life
Where there is beauty, the beauty of growth

To Be a Bridge

There are times in our lives
Times such as these
When we can be
The bridge
Must be the bridge
The bridge to love and light
To hope and peace
To connection
To healing
And to become a bridge
It doesn't take much
It takes pausing
It takes listening
It takes seeing and hearing
It takes knowing this matters
This moment matters
Knowing transformation is possible
In this moment
There is a way
There is a bridge
To change the story
In this moment

The Little Things

There are times
When death becomes our teacher
Always reminding us
That the little things matter
The way we say hello
What we notice or fail to notice
Hearing what is being said
And what is not being said
It is the little things that matter
The sound of someone's voice
The look in their eye
The power of touch
The softness of a smile
It is the little things that matter
Holding a hand
The grace of holding a story
Of holding the truth
Of holding space
It is the little things that matter
Choosing kindness
The way we say goodbye
What we remember
The gratitude
That grows in the heart
When we know
What hurts the most

Is what mattered the most
And it was
The little things

Death as a Teacher

When death comes
It is not the end
Oh, it may be the end of this life
Of this being
Of this chapter
But for those left to carry on
For those who write the next chapter
A death is turning the page
It is an opportunity
To remember
To change and grow
It is a teacher
A teacher of what matters most
It is the beginning
Of understanding life
It is a place
To begin again

It's Okay to Not Know

I have been one
Who wanted certainty
Who needed certainty
Or at least
I thought I did
But
It seems I've been mistaken
And in reality
It's okay to not know
To have doubts and questions
Even despair
It's okay to take what your heart needs
And to leave the rest
If you believe in love
Believe in love
If you believe in hope
Believe in hope
If you believe in peace
Believe in peace
If you believe in healing
Believe in healing
And if you need to ask questions
Ask questions
It's okay to not know

Presence

Sometimes
It's hard to be the quiet one
To want to be the wise one
The one with all the answers
The funny one
Keeping everyone entertained
But, then
It's good to remember
There are times
When it's so good
To just be present
And to be truly present
You have to wait
There has to be silence
You have to allow the silence
And then there is the possibility
Of catching the story
Of seeing
Of hearing
Of knowing
This matters
Whoever is in front of you
They matter

Something to Practice

I read the other day
That happiness is a practice
And that
Has been a "game changer"
What if we practice being happy
Practice appreciating what we have
When we have it
Practice being grateful
Practice being at peace
Practice being curious
Practice being love
Practice being the change
It's like anything else
That we practice
The more we practice
The better we get
So why not practice
Being happy
Giving yourself permission
To get better
At happiness
It could be
The beginning of the rest of your life

To Change

I had to smile
And then laugh
When I read
"In order to change
You have to make changes"
What a concept
You have to change
In order to change
Even, especially, when it's hard
In order to be brave
You have to do things that scare you
You have to speak your truth
You have to disagree respectfully
In order to love
You have to do loving things
You have to forgive, listen, grow, change, be kind
In order to be connected
You have to do things that create connection
You have to show up
To see, to listen, to hear
In order to be happy
You have to allow happiness
In order to be healthy
You have to live a healthy life
In order to be free
You have to allow differences

You have to know everyone matters
You have to let go
In order to change
You have to surrender

Sometimes

Sometimes
What scares you the most
Is what you want the most
Sometimes
Letting go
Is where you find a place to hold on
Reaching the end
Is a place to start over
Falling down
Is a place to get back up
Sometimes
Saying good-bye
Is a place to say hello
Surrendering
Is a place to breathe again
And sometimes
Giving up one way of life
Is where new life begins

About the Author

Anne is a writer, a Life Cycle Celebrant, and a hospice nurse. She holds a master's degree in hospice education and bereavement. She has three children and three grandchildren. She lost her youngest son to suicide. That loss often guides her in her work and her writing. Anne lives in Michigan.

www.ingramcontent.com/pod-product-compliance
Lightning Source LLC
LaVergne TN
LVHW020640100826
845148LV00012B/2256

* 9 7 9 8 2 3 4 0 8 4 9 9 6 *